UNREST:
No Place For Peace

ED H. SMITH

UNREST: No Place For Peace
All Rights Reserved.
Copyright © 2018 Ed H. Smith
v6.0 r2.0

The opinions expressed in this manuscript are solely the opinions of the author and do not represent the opinions or thoughts of the publisher. The author has represented and warranted full ownership and/or legal right to publish all the materials in this book.

This book may not be reproduced, transmitted, or stored in whole or in part by any means, including graphic, electronic, or mechanical without the express written consent of the publisher except in the case of brief quotations embodied in critical articles and reviews.

Printed under CAJAKES

ISBN: 978-0-578-20325-6

Cover Photo © 2018 Ed H. Smith. All rights reserved - used with permission.

PRINTED IN THE UNITED STATES OF AMERICA

Dedicated to my wife,
Carolyn A. Smith

Based partially on facts.

Table of Contents

The Sentencing of James Ford Seale	1
How It All Started	7
Who Killed Jim Keys?	11
Who Killed A.D. Brown?	20
Who Hanged Johnny Nix in Jail?	27
The Killings of Charles Eddie Moore and Henry Hezekiah Dee	29
Killing Blacks in Mississippi Was Easy	41
Losing Minnie Lee was a Crushing Blow	64
Black Pillars in the Local Community	71
White Pillars in the Local Community	76
Moving Forward	82

The Sentencing of James Ford Seale

I was sitting in a courtroom with my niece, Sandy Glow, in Jackson, Mississippi the summer of 2007. I was dumbfounded after years of killings of black people and nothing was ever done to bring white killers to trial.

Reflecting on racial events during the forties and early fifties, I realized that something was grossly wrong with a system of government that allowed white people to do whatever harm they wished to black people without punishment.

We waited eagerly for the judge to sentence James Ford Seale, a white Ku Klux Klan member, for the kidnapping, conspiracy and brutal killings of two young black men, Charles Eddie Moore, whom we called Nub, and Henry Hezekiah Dee. Their beatings and near murders took place forty-three years prior in the Homochitto Forest near Meadville, Mississippi. No matter how harsh Ford's sentence, it would not be justifiable for the crimes he and his co-conspirators committed against Moore and Dee.

The friends and family members in the courtroom had come hoping for the harshest possible sentence for James Ford Seale. In reality, we weren't expecting him to get hard labor or extended time because he was white and the system always favored white people. However, this time, our inner fears came to a very positive fruition. The judge gave Seale three life sentences which meant he would die in jail.

He looked old, worn out, exhausted, thin and frail, slightly bent over and moved as if the end of life for him was near. What I had heard of him caused me to form the opinion that he was the embodiment of sleaziness and the profound representation of Satan. On the scale of human dignity and purity, I would place him at the same level as the bottom of an aged old privy.

Attentively, I listened for him to say his heartfelt solemn words of "I'm sorry for what I've done to the deceased and their families," to try and garner a bit of leniency for himself. He never uttered such words, proving he wasn't sorry for the horrendous crimes he committed. He didn't look remorseful at all and his mannerism still portrayed him as the big man in the pack of scoundrels in which he once yielded awesome power.

The harsh and muscular panoply of criminals that once availed themselves to his malicious indulgence left him without support to face the forceful clutches of justice. There was no white knight band of ferocious killers to snatch him from the vise of justice to scurry him to a KKK sanctuary as in the Homochitto Forest for safety.

A prudent jury in Jackson, Mississippi had done to him what should have been done years earlier in Meadville, Mississippi. They found a white man guilty of kidnapping and conspiracy of two black men. After forty-three years, Seale still hobbled his vicious killer mannerism, exemplifying no remorse whatsoever for the deadly atrocities he committed against Moore and Dee.

The Judge granted Command Sergeant Major Thomas James Moore, Charles Eddie Moore's older brother, a chance to read his statement to Seale. Thomas James Moore, who had given his entire adult life to the military, read his deeply touching and gripping statement. It moved me to delve into the Moore and Dee killings as well as other black killings that took place years earlier in and around Meadville.

I wanted people to understand why those blacks were killed, who killed them, and what happened to the killers. I wondered if there was an adverse impact from the killings on the town and the people, black and white. I wanted to know the people's reactions. Specially, I wanted to learn as much about the Moore and Dee killings as possible and all participants involved and why. I wondered if I could find anyone that could or would talk to me about these murders.

Over the years, I connoted in my mind that people who hated or killed black people for no apparent reasons were either, scurrilous, narcissistic, or sycophantic, or all three. The sheer refines of human nature, the do the right things, the accepted moral tones of a deity were never innate or developed in their souls. What seemed apparent was genuinely and solely perversely engraved on their brains, without a scintilla of morality. The depth of one's Godliness will determine how far he will stray from what is right. If the right thing is not internalized, the right thing will not be effectuated.

I wanted to know if Moore and Dee were on a list of blacks to be killed and if so, why were they targets? I also wondered if there were other blacks on a list to be picked up by the Klan and killed. It is hard to believe that there was a plan to pick up Moore and Dee and torture them for certain information and ultimately allow them to walk free. I can't see such a thing happening. My goal was get all the facts possible and put them in a book for the entire world to read forever. The public needs to know as much about those cases as possible.

The crimes are too horrendous, heinous, and vicious just to say that Moore and Dee and others were killed and let their cases die just because they were black. Something needs to be said, something needs to be done. Someone should've stood up and yelled for justice.

If a black person killed a rabbit, squirrel or deer out of season and got caught in Mississippi, that person would certainly end up in trouble, heavily fined and license taken. His action would be criminal and that person could go to jail.

I know Mississippi very well and I understand maliciousness and social traditions, but for the life of me,

I've never understood hate, violence, brutality and crime, against black folk without any provocation whatsoever. The only thing that I can garner from the hate factor is, just because certain people are black and defenseless, they receive injustice.

I wanted to find someone who could and would talk to me about the killings or point me to someone that would sit down with me and discuss the cases. I hoped that person had enough facts to identify the individuals involved, no matter how minuscule or extensive their knowledge was.

I am seriously bothered because I cannot figure out just what it is that makes certain white people hate black people and will go to extreme measures to do them bodily harm even though they have not been harmed in any manner by a single black person. I wonder what stimuli it took to forage the devastating thought of murder into the head of Seale and for him to magnetize others to get involved with him in committing such Lucifer driven acts against two innocent people that they didn't even know, had never heard of or met, not even once.

During my growing up in Mississippi, I met some people that were very noteworthy. Some are black people that I considered pillars in the community that lived and survived the travails of abuse in order just to survive. There were also white people that I considered pillars in the community that exhibited integrity and decency and refused to heap belligerency on black people or relegate them into a position of submission to whites just because they were black. They did not diminish their character and stoop to the level of sadists just to be in good standing with haters of black people.

Such hateful acts happened in the county, in the town of Meadville, in the county jail, in the Homochitto Forest and in one case, a private black home. I wanted all my information to be fair, honest and correct. After all, I was born in Franklin County, Mississippi and there I grew up. It is where I attained the infrastructure of my life. Even though I've been away for years, I am happiest when I go home. I still call Franklin County, Meadville, Kirby and Roxie Mississippi home.

How It All Started

It was a pleasure to read the history of Meadville when I started researching the town. All that it took to build and maintain Meadville was people working together with one goal in mind for the good of the people and the town project. It is a good example for young people to read, learn and emulate.

When I was in the ninth grade at Mount Olive Colored School, I was told by a friend that Meadville got its name from Cowles Meade, a former Governor and Secretary of territory and Speaker of the House in the U.S. Congress.

At one point, Meadville was a hot spot and gathering place for politicians and business people as well as various other professionals. Later, it went through an economic downturn and major rehabs of various buildings had to be done.

The real redevelopment push came from a lot of foreigners that migrated and settled in Meadville. They were from

Europe, Russia, and Latin America. They brought with them people with cognitive skills, resources, money and commitments to invest in the town and they reared families and built businesses. Apparently, they gleaned through keen insight that Meadville could have a long, positive future and that they should adhere, participate and be productive in the reconstruction for a strong economy. They weren't driven by greed but were resourceful, good business people with resilience. Some were doctors, lawyers, mechanics and skilled workers. Some eventually set up shops themselves and became the prominent business people of the town. They put down their roots and seeds, and germination took roots and yielded expansion and growth in the town.

Because the foreigners perceived a great future in the town, they committed to stay and work together and apply their resources for improving Meadville and it became a thriving town again and the county seat of Franklin County.

Today, Meadville is a modern town with a telephone system, a bank, school system, water and sewer system, businesses and churches, post office with paved streets, and a major highway connecting it to east, west, north and south of the United States.

However, during later years, small minds, bigotry, racism, and viciousness against black people have scarred the face of Meadville with degrees of debauchery more treacherous and heinous than one could imagine. Nowhere is it written, talked about or surmised that the foreigners or their offspring in Franklin County ever adapted such mindsets of calamities to associate themselves with any form of maliciousness that was leveled against blacks in Meadville or Franklin County.

In the early forties and fifties, some black folk in Franklin County lived daily in constant fear and agony wondering what could or would happen to them and their families. Black folk were relegated to white submissiveness. Blacks were prohibited from even a minute form of positive changes in justice and liberty. There were ugly and vicious attitudes that existed and perpetrated among a cadre of unsavory characters that were so camouflaged within the community that it went completely unnoticed. Their activities were unknown even by close family members and their neighbors that lived next door. Those characters existed for years and people, in general, didn't know of their activities.

That vicious group is called the Ku Klux Klan. They were dangerously savage and mostly nocturnal in their sporadic criminal indulgence, but their attacks certainly weren't ephemeral. If they had issues with a black person and wanted to do that person bodily harm, they would abduct him and scurry that victim to their secluded place off the beaten path to unmercifully gang beat him or hang him to a tree. If that person was allowed to live, but ordered out of Franklin County immediately, that was exactly what they meant. That person might not be allowed to go home for a change of clothes, but pointed towards the railroad track, highway or wooded trail, and someone yelled, "Run. Don't look back or stop and never come back!"

An objectionable black person to the rules of the Klan had three choices: Be quiet, be submissive or be gone. One thing was for sure, the Klan was mean. They didn't laugh or play, and were meaner than rattle snakes. Blacks knew it, abhorred it, but couldn't change its existence.

They killed people and got away with not even a slap on the wrist because they were the Klan, white, and in control of all the power.

Who Killed Jim Keys?

Here's what I found out about the Keys killing.

His daughter said that Jim Keys was a quiet man, well-mannered, and very popular. He wore khaki pants or Hercules overalls during the week that were always starched and pressed. He dressed up with matching attire including shoes and socks. His cap or hat matched everything that he wore. On Sundays, he was always the best-dressed man in the church, wearing a nice-looking suit with a tie and shined shoes. Jim was so well coordinated that people called him Black Satin as an affectionate nick name attributed to his chicly dress. He had several gold teeth that regularly flashed when he smiled.

Jim was a very handsome man, with a well-shaped physique and strong muscle tones. His mingle gray hair was always neatly trimmed with a part to the left side. He was soft spoken, even when he laughed. His character was laden with dignity. It was his style and he never digressed from that position.

He attended Sunday school regularly at Mt. Olive Baptist Church. They only had church service once each month. Jim served on the deacon board. When the deacons held their meetings, he was always in attendance and worked to help bring to fruition whatever they discussed that would be good for the church. Jim was incredibly easy to work with and if he committed, he honored his commitment. He was always on time with anything in which he was involved.

Jim had a special love for children and was always buying things for them from dolls to bicycles, along with candy and cookies and other special treats for Christmas and holidays. He cared about older people, and if one was in need, Jim was always ready to step in and help with whatever was needed.

Jim was a loner. He never remarried after his wife Etta died. His two children lived with another family. He wasn't sociable, even when he was around very close relatives or friends. He had no close friends with whom he spent a lot of time or shared information. He did not party at a juke joint during the weekends. Jim didn't drink or smoke or use profane language. He didn't get into anyone's business, and he didn't allow anyone to get into his. He was always pleasant and helped anyone in need.

Jim was a proud black man as he took pride in standing on his own two feet. He demanded respect in the manner that he carried himself from everyone that knew him. He treated everyone right. He made no differences among black people and he stood up to whites, looked them in the eyes and responded to them as a man.

Some people said that Jim was a bootlegger of illegal whiskey. That was hearsay. People didn't know if Jim had a distillery or if he was a distributor of whiskey. Some said that he distributed his whiskey as far away as Vidalia and Ferriday, Louisiana. Whatever Jim was doing, it was lucrative, and he did it for years clandestinely and never was arrested for anything that was outside of the law.

He never flaunted his money or talked about how he made his living. His quiet mannerism and low-keyed style were apparently what made him successful.

Black people who had enough money to have a bank account refused to put their money in a bank because they didn't trust white bank employees. If blacks had money, they didn't want white people to know it nor how much they really had.

Jim was no such person, he was wealthy, had a bank account with substantial dollars in a savings account and hundreds of dollars in a checking account. Even though he had much more money than he deposited, he wanted to have a bank account to pay his property taxes and when he was ready to purchase a different truck, he had a banking history and could do so without a problem.

It was rumored that Jim had a hidden distillery way back in the woods and had been selling bootleg whiskey for years, but was never caught. People claimed that he made the best whiskey of all the people that had been in the business over the years. No one knew how he got started in the business but they speculated that if he was in the business, he picked up the trade from his granddaddy who some people claim had been in the distiller business until he died.

Rumor had it that Jim's granddad left him thousands of dollars and that he knew how to manage it without giving the impression that he was well-off. He dressed as everyone else that had a steady job. He owned nothing extra that would set him in a class all by himself. He drove a pickup truck that was always three to four years old and reliable. He never carried around a lot of money, just enough to take care of his needs for the day.

Jim had a house, a mule, and a horse, two cows, a bull and chickens, and each year he grew a variety of truck crops. His vegetable crops yielded substantially each year and Jim was seen in Natchez, Brookhaven, and McComb regularly during the summer delivering vegetable to customers that he had built up over the years.

If he was a whiskey dealer, the vegetables and eggs he sold gave him a good cover for the dollars he took in from illegal whiskey dealings.

It was said that Jim Keys never sold whiskey around where he lived or around the Mile Branch or across the railroad track. He never placed himself in a precarious position, but somehow the unfortunate happened. He was beaten to near death in his house and left unconscious. How someone got into his home and viciously attacked him was never known. It was bizarre that he was attacked because he was so cautious about his safety and security. People thought he never let his guard down.

The entire facts around his case never got to his family, just unofficial bits and pieces about what people heard. I think the reason there were no facts was because the people who were supposed to investigate the crime didn't care about finding the criminal. Jim Keys was black, and his killer or killers were purported to be white. White murderers of blacks did not get charged.

Everyone thought that Jim was killed for the money that he was making and he had the audacity and was bold enough not to have someone white protect him and give him permission to do what he was doing illegally. To make big money and refuse to pay protection coverage just didn't happen. Everyone knew that the sheriff of the town called the shots. Even in the surrounding towns, the owners of small businesses that sold whiskey had to pay up or they couldn't sell the whiskey.

The Klan and vicious racists whites knew that the bullet or billy club they used to kill a black or the tree branch they used to hang him was worth more to them than the life of a dead black person. The value of a black life didn't exceed that of a favorite house pet and certainly not that of a farm animal.

Similar to the Underground Railroad, the black grapevine was very sophisticated in getting secret information from white people without them knowing. They had no surveillance or high-tech equipment but black cleaning workers, cooks, drivers, yard and field hands quietly working around white folk with their eyes and ears open. If they heard something of value, they cataloged it and later, passed it on to other blacks at night. The next day, they went right back to work just as if they knew nothing.

Jim lived across the railroad tracks a little northeast of the Mile Branch. The back of his house was a short distance from Middle Folk Creek. People couldn't believe that someone got close enough to beat him to near death in his own house. There were whisperings and suggestions that two white men were the culprits, however, no one was ever positively identified or charged.

Black folk believed that either the sheriff knew who the offenders were or had him beaten up himself. The theory was, Jim wouldn't pay the Sheriff a protection fee which angered him and he had Jim beaten up. Those were just thoughts, there were no known facts.

There was another theory that some fellows named Willard Smith and his friend called Cook may have beaten Jim up during a robbery attempt, however, there was no evidence.

The family had tried to get Jim to allow someone to live with him, but he rejected the very idea because he did not want anyone to be that close to him in case someone attempted to do him harm, but he paid with his life.

A friend kept him in her home in an unconscious state until he died, never getting from him who attacked him.

On the day of his funeral, the church was jam packed

with people, many of whom were white. This was surprising to every black person in attendance. No one knew that Jim had those kinds of contacts with that many white people. People knew some of Jim's contacts, but they didn't think he had dealings with so many white people that would give up their day to come to a black man's funeral. Most of the white people that were there weren't known to the black congregation of the church. That meant that Jim had established stable relationships with them in his business dealings somewhere along the lines. Two white people, a woman, and a man spoke when the pastor gave time for the community to talk.

The white woman said that her name was July Sommers and that she had known Jim for years and had done business with him just as long. He supplied her and her husband and their business with vegetable for years, and they never had a bad batch of anything, and he was always on time. He was an honest business man and was fair with his prices. She and her husband were shocked to hear of this tragedy. Mrs. Sommers went on to say that they will miss Jim and it is regrettable that this could happen to such a fine gentleman.

The white man said, "I have known Jim for a lot of years and I have never heard of anyone saying that Jim ever had done one thing wrong to anyone. You might find what I'm about to say shocking, but Jim was my friend for a long time, and I know he was a good man. If one needed it, he would give the shirt off of his back. He bothered no one, but he would help anyone. I hope that the responsible person is found and justice is served. The killer or killers, black or white, should be in jail forever."

The people couldn't believe what they were hearing, but what they heard from the white speakers were pleasing to their ears. No one in the community had ever heard Jim talk about any white people that he knew or had seen any of them ever dealing with him.

Generally, when blacks dealt in illegal whiskey, only one close family member knew the details. The wives and children were kept out of and away from the operation. They weren't told about the inner workings of the distilleries. This was done because if the local sheriff or more prominent law enforcement officers found owners at the distilleries making whiskey, they killed them in their effort to escape. The family was kept away for safety reasons.

The way dealers sold their whiskey was unique. Each sale was placed in a different location and buyers were told where to find it. They collected their money before the whiskey was picked up. They never left the whiskey to be picked up in the same place twice and they always delivered the whiskey to the pickup spot at night. Their ideal delivery time was midnight. They always went to the distilleries in different directions just in case someone was watching. The worst the weather conditions, the happier the distillery owner.

An owner never went directly to his distillery from home. They sat around on the periphery for some time to make sure that the law was not waiting for them to arrive.

Only when they were sure that there wasn't any movement or sound around the distillery did they approach the operation. They were smart operators and their smarts kept them alive and out of trouble and jail.

In spite of black folk's efforts and plans to stay free and away from the law, every now and then the law ended up sneaking up on the distillery and killing some black dealer. That happened because someone got second-hand information and shot off their mouth, and ultimately the law found out what was going on, searched and found the distillery and killed the owner.

Who Killed A.D. Brown?

The new effort to embellish the town of Meadville by the newcomers from various parts of the world did not only include sprucing up town businesses, but also the construction of a new jail which ultimately became a place of disgust and disgrace. A brutal killing place for a young black man named A.D. Brown.

A.D. Brown was a fine young man as well as a very handsome fellow. He was a good child coming up and adhered to the direction of his parents by not getting into trouble. He respected older people and helped them when they had a problem and called on him.

In school, he was the quiet one in the crowd that girls mostly admired, not only for his good looks, but for his maturity. A.D.'s development surpassed that of his peers and friends. He was level headed in his approach to everything. Gentlemanly was always his style. He had lots of friends that admired him for his good qualities. He was an impressive, very disciplined and positive fellow for his age.

A.D. loved to earn his own money and had no reservation about working. Hard work or long hours didn't bother him, but he always got an agreement up front as to how much he was going to get paid and that is what he expected to receive on payday. He went to work on time every day and did his job according to the rules and never fluffed off. He did his work and he demanded his pay. If he didn't get paid according to the agreement, he quit, no matter who or where he was working. He never argued with whom he worked and respected them as his employer, but demanded respect in the way he carried himself.

In the final analysis, his integrity and will power cost him his life in the most vicious way inside the Meadville Franklin County jail under lock and key. He was beaten to death.

White people in Franklin County in the early fifties demanded that blacks be totally submissive to them and their wishes. What they wanted from blacks, they expected to get without questions. They didn't expect blacks to try and negotiate anything positive for themselves. What white people offered blacks were expected to be accepted, shut up and work. Not a single question was to be asked by a black person.

The first black that was killed in the Meadville jail was A.D. Brown. They said that A.D. Brown had been working for a farmer out near the Rose Hill community about twelve miles from downtown Meadville, Mississippi.

Apparently, A.D. Brown was not paid the amount the farm owner had agreed to pay him. A.D. refused to work and walked away.

It is surmised that the farmer indicated to the sheriff of Meadville that Brown had taken something of value from his farm and should be arrested. On the day of the detention, Brown was sitting on the Bank of Franklin's steps in Meadville where some people would sit after working hours. The Sheriff saw him and made the arrest and placed him in jail. That would be the last time A.D. Brown's feet would touch the ground.

It was discovered that, while in jail, someone came to him during the night and A.D. reiterated his stance not to work unless he was paid what he was promised. At that point, the beating commenced. He was savagely bludgeoned to death.

I can't imagine the horror of his beating death. Brains scattered across the jail floor, eyes knocked out, arms broken, ribs crushed, teeth knocked out, face caved in, and hands smashed. They said that blood was everywhere as if the jail was a slaughtering floor for butchering animals. I can't fathom even at a minuscule level that there are individuals in our humane society having such inhumane, violent tendencies that they would commit such a wanton act and live with themselves. I don't understand how any person with a heart, no matter how mean-spirited he might be, could do such a thing, look at himself in the mirror and call himself a human being. It is utterly befuddling.

During hog killing time in Mississippi, people didn't mutilate the hog to be killed, they either hit it on the head once with a mallet and cut his throat or they shot him once. The hog kill was not brutal. A.D. was murdered much worse than an animal. The sadist behind his killing hated him, mind, soul, and body. The killers' tendencies were perpetual and didn't die with the assassination of A.D., they remained intact for the next kill.

In the first place, whoever got into the jail had to have the permission of someone with a key. That being understood, everyone with access to keys should have been investigated to the fullest and charges brought against them starting with the sheriff. The question was, who would investigate when everyone connected is wrapped in the same sheet.

One Klan member, even if he is the sheriff, does not investigate another. In other words, a racists white sheriff does not snitch on a fellow member. They were all members of the same murderous, vicious hate team and they protected each other.

People were saying that a black man was brought into the jail to beat A.D. Brown. Blacks didn't believe that to be true. If it was true, it was because a gun was pointed at his head and he did it to save his own life. I am black and I know black people. What was done to A.D. wasn't by a black person. Don't believe such a lie.

Under no circumstances should anyone not connected officially to the jail have keys. The killing was committed supposedly by an outside force with a key to the jail cell. If that was true, the sheriff was connected to the murder. Someone should have to answer for the killing by a legitimate inquiring body. It should not have been swept under the rug and forgotten.

It appears to me that the department of justice either didn't know about the killing or didn't care that a poor black man was beaten to death in a Mississippi jail. Maybe his death was not significant to them, or they didn't want to face the reality of southern racism, or personnel was asleep or overlooked their responsibilities. Perhaps they didn't want to get involved in justice for a black man in Mississippi. If A.D. Brown had been a white man, the President of the United States would have screamed for justice and it would have been served immediately.

The gravity of grief the family must have gone through as a result of the dreadful death of A.D., had to have been an abjection beyond comprehension. I can understand a parent in Meadville, Mississippi going to bed praying for a miracle that would free a son from the town jail when there is no trust in the people in charge. Yet, as vicious as some southern law enforcement people were, the idea of your child being beaten to death in the jail was unthinkable.

In the first place, one wouldn't think it was possible even if someone wanted to kill A.D. while incarcerated. A hater would believe that it's too blatant to take the chance to kill someone in jail. The sheriff would be looked at immediately with a jaundiced eye. To commit murder in the town jail, no way, they wouldn't have the gall. A black man might be tried unjustly and convicted by a biased jury and given an extended, or even a death sentence, but to have your child murdered in jail is unbelievable. As horribly dangerous and horrific as it was for blacks, killing someone in jail just wasn't believed to happen.

The sheriff probably didn't say anything to his staff the morning after A.D. Brown was beaten to death in the jail next door to where they worked. On second thought, I suspect he said nothing to the local newspaper, nothing to the business people, and nothing to the Brown family. Just that he's dead.

The crime should not have been allowed to be skirted. It was too brazen and too contemptuous. The issue should have been raised with the national government.

For the record, whoever was involved in the brutal murder of A.D. will have their trial in the court of judgment, and they can't walk away with a "not guilty" plea. Only those without a spot or wrinkle will be able to stand that trial. Those killers will pay in the end.

A.D.'s family could only huddle in pathos. They didn't know how to proceed and had no protection. The fear they experienced had to be traumatic because they knew exactly what would happen to each of them if one word got out that they were talking to higher authorities regarding the killing of A.D.

Mississippi was one of the most disgraceful states in the union because of the shameful ways blacks were treated.

Black people wondered if Mississippi would ever change. Surviving among white people was like walking on window panes in cleats while holding heavy weights. You could never let your guard down, if so, within a second, one's life could change to trouble or calamity.

During early 1950s in Mississippi, racism was a barricade for any tangible upward progress for black people. During this same period, young blacks began changing their responses to white people. Courtesy and respect were given to all older people, black and white along with the customary "yes ma'am" or "sir." It was evident to younger white men and women that Blacks were communicating by the usage of "yes" or "no" responses or in a circumlocutory manner to avoid being submissive.

Young black people were changing all around, going to college, the military, Chicago, New York, and Detroit, where they were free and gained progressive experience that was passed back to their relatives still living in Mississippi. They started to change by not going to the back door of restaurants to get a sandwich, or going to the second floor to see a movie. Amos and Andy, who were whites imitating black characters, were no longer their weekly radio show.

I guess people thought what happened in the 1950s wouldn't occur in the 1960s. However, it did and the murders were more vicious than ever.

Who Hanged Johnny Nix in Jail?

Johnny Nix was hanged in jail. From what I understood, he should not have been in jail in the first place. Well, as a native Mississippian, I learned early on that there was one thing that could get a black person in jail any time of day, any time of night or any day of the week. That was for any white person to say, "I want black Joe locked up." He didn't give a reason. He gave a statement and Black Joe was going to be locked up immediately. The only way Black Joe could avoid being locked up was to get out of Mississippi or have a white sponsor. Not one person, black or white was going to protest Black Joe being locked up.

No one could tell me why Johnny Nix should have been in jail or what crime he had committed. I tried to find a close relative, friend or someone that knew him. I garnered nothing.

I tried to find out where Johnny was born, where he went to school, where he worked. I tried to find out with whom he associated, where he spent his leisure time and anything that would allow me to learn something about him.

In my search, I finally did learn of a person who knew volumes about him. I attempted to contact that person through someone that I knew. All to no avail. The response I got back was an emphatic "No!"

That's what I got from every one I attempted to talk to about Johnny Nix.

From what I could garner, neither Johnny nor A.D. was afraid of white people. They looked them in the eyes, stood up straight and spoke up as men. Their styles were not the norm in Mississippi and maybe that's what caused them their deaths.

The Killings of Charles Eddie Moore and Henry Hezekiah Dee

During the early 1960s two of the most horrific killings that ever happened to black people were committed by several Ku Klux Klan members in Mississippi.

They committed the crime in the Homochitto Forest off the Bunkley Road west of Meadville, Mississippi in Franklin County. The two murdered young men were Henry Hezekiah Dee and Charles Eddie Moore.

I remember Moore as that gregarious and affable kid with a courteous mannerism, and Henry Dee with his lovely white teeth and smooth skin who loved to kid around with other kids at school. Dee was a calm and playful child who got along with others. I gathered that he garnered his mannerism from his grandmother, Mrs. Honey we called her. She was a very nice lady and was a member of Mt. Olive church where she brought her children and grandchildren to service, including Henry Dee.

Both Moore and Dee were fine young men with stellar backgrounds. They had no records of crimes, misgivings, or involvement with members of any gang in Chicago.

Only Dee had ever lived in Chicago and attended Farragut High School for a short time. He never joined any groups while in Chicago and he didn't live in the Black Panthers' area.

However, Klan member, Charles Marcus Edwards, labeled Henry Dee as a Black Panther and conduit for running guns into Meadville and Franklin County from Chicago. He said Dee was a Chicago Black Panther whose aim was to organize black people in Franklin County and create a mechanism to kill white people and to move black people into a position of control in Franklin County. The authentication of his position was that Dee had lived in Chicago, wore a black bandanna, and had a conked hair style, which was regularly worn by black entertainers as well as other common black people.

Dee once lived about a mile from me, and we attended Mt. Olive High school. Our families belonged to Mt. Olive Missionary Baptist Church in Kirby, a farming area. I knew both Dee and Moore's families. We called Moore's mother, cousin Mazie and Dee's mom, Icyphine.

Moore attended Lillie May Bryant High School in Meadville where he was the center on the football team.

Mack Litterton, the quarterback, saw Moore as a small aggressive center that wouldn't back down from the defender in front of him no matter how large he may have been. He took him on with all the vengeance that he could muster. His ferocious tackles probably shocked the opposition because with his small statue, he wasn't expected to have the charge he exemplified. It was his fight and heart he delivered.

In May, 1964, Moore and Dee were hitching a ride at the intersection of 84 highway and McNair Road near the corporate city limits of Meadville, Mississippi. Meadville is in the southwest corner of Franklin County, about thirty-two miles from Natchez, Mississippi. They were hitching in the direction they both lived.

Moore lived about four miles west from Meadville and Dee may have been going all the way to Roxie, Mississippi where his family lived which was about eleven miles west of Meadville, if he wasn't going home with Moore.

It was said that James Ford Seale and Charles Marcus Edward were riding together when they saw Moore and Dee hitching. James Ford Seale stopped and picked them up under the pretense he was a government revenue agent investigating moonshine whiskey distilleries in the area and wanted to talk to them about that. In addition, he said he wanted them to meet other agents working in the area. Moore and Dee just wanted a ride.

After a short distance, Charles Marcus Edwards got out of Seale's car and into his own automobile and followed Seale. Somewhere along the way, James Ford Seale brandished a gun while forcibly driving Moore and Dee several miles away from Meadville and into the Homochitto Forest where he tied them to trees.

Klan members were convened on the site and they made a decision to beat the gun information they wanted out of them. The Klan members took turns beating Moore and Dee near death, trying to get them to confess.

Dee and Moore responded numerous times during the beatings that they had no weapons and didn't know of anyone who did. The beatings continued until Dee, to gain relief, finally told them that the guns were hidden in the Roxie Baptist Church.

The Klan members got a search warrant signed by Sheriff Hutto, who was said to have a connection to the Klan. They searched the church and found no guns. It was said that James Ford Seale became extremely mercurial and went into a frenzy, exercising a savage personality. The beatings resumed. Moore and Dee begged for their lives to no avail.

One story that was floated around was that Moore and Dee were beaten for the rest of the day after they were picked up. Another is that they were beaten for two days and with just a fraction of life left.

The members realized they weren't going to get any substantive information from Dee and Moore and decided they would dump them into a tributary leading to the Mississippi River. It was said that no Klan member at the beating site knew how to get to the spot in the tributary where the bodies could be dropped to reach the river. However, someone knew of a Klan member who did.

Apparently, Clyde Seale, the father of James Ford Seale, called Jack Seale who lived in Natchez, Mississippi. He told him he wanted him involved in what they were doing and advised him to have Earl Parker, who also lived in Natchez, to call him.

Clyde wanted Earl to come to the Homochitto Forest spot. Earl Parker had a boat docked at the tributary site called the Palmyra. Earl met Clyde and others at the Homochitto Forest where they held Dee and Moore. Earl also gave James Ford Seale, Jack and Edwards an old Jeep motor block to chain to Henry Dee and parts of old train rails to chain to Moore. This site must have been a regular meeting place for the Klan, otherwise, how would Earl Parker have known where to meet Clyde Seale?

It was stated that Earl Parker seemed to know the back woods of the Mississippi River between Tallulah, Louisiana and Natchez, Mississippi and was aware of the area because it was one of his favorite fishing spots. He specifically gave instructions to James Ford Seale regarding where to dump the bodies. It was also stated that Parker did not go to the tributary site. Moore and Dee were loaded into the trunk of Parker's automobile and driven almost one hundred miles to be dumped into the Mississippi river.

They drove through Vicksburg, Mississippi and west across the Mississippi River through Tallulah, Louisiana and south down the Mississippi River to the Palmyra tributary.

Moore and Dee's brutally beaten bodies were loaded into a boat and taken out into the deep water, chained and weighed down, but still alive and dumped into the stream. That dastardly, murderous act was as surreal and malicious as any individual can stoop.

James Ford Seale was asked at the trial why he dumped Moore and Dee in the river still alive. His response was:

"I would've shot them, but I didn't want to get blood in the boat."

James Ford Seale had a vicious background as indicated in the shotgun beating of Alton Alford and it is believed that he was involved in the killing of a man named Hodges.

Some people suggested that Seale was involved, along with Raleigh Glover, in the assassination of the NAACP member Wharlest Jackson and the attempted murder of George Metcalfe, President of the Natchez NAACP and Reverend Clyde Briggs of Roxie, Mississippi.

It is said that Raleigh Glover was the founder of the Silver Dollar Group and a most belligerent militant member.

The word is that between 1964 and 1967, at least six black men were killed by the Klan, but there was only one conviction, Dee and Moore and that took forty-three years.

Had it not been for Thomas James Moore, Charles Moore's brother, who got involved, James Ford Seale may never have been convicted. The discovery that Moore and Dee were severely beaten on federal land was pivotal.

The word is that Seale was not tried for the murders of Dee and Moore in Meadville, Mississippi for the lack of evidence. However, blacks in Mississippi would not expect an all-white jury, white lawyers and a white judge in the sixties to find a white person guilty for killing blacks. That was the way of the South. There was *no place for peace* for a black person.

Initially, when Moore and Dee didn't come home for several days, their families went to Sheriff Wayne Hutto's office in Meadville, Mississippi for help. The Sheriff told them he would look into the matter.

After several more days, the parents checked back with Sheriff Hutto and he told them that he had found them alive and well in some town near New Orleans, Louisiana. He told them to go home and not to worry, the boys were fine. However, he didn't give any specifics. No phone number, no address and no family name as to where Moore and Dee were staying.

I garnered from the Sheriff's statement that he knew what had already happened and his lies made him complicit in the cover-up. Who knows, he may have been part of the act. After all, he had been visited by Klan members to obtain a warrant to search the Roxie Baptist Church for guns and ammunition.

Sheriff Wayne Hutto was labeled by some people as part of the Klan and was just as low life and guilty as James Ford Seale, Clyde Seale, and Earl Parker. Hutto was the chief law enforcement officer in Meadville, Mississippi. He was a disgrace to the town and to the office of the Sheriff. He lied to the parents of Dee and Moore because he didn't want them bothering him for help in finding their sons. He just wanted them to leave and never return.

The principal impediment for me is to know how Charles Marcus Edwards surmised that Henry Dee was a Black Panther, all because he wore a bandana and conked hair style. I later found out that Charles Marcus Edwards was a dedicated Klansman who wanted to be part of murdering Moore and Dee. He also claimed that his wife saw Dee urinating near his house and for that, he was angry with him.

Say what you think, but God sees all, and he moves justifiably. It is inexplicably clear that Henry Dee and Charles Moore were killed without provocation. They were killed because they were black by cruel, haters of all black folks. The KKK's goal was about preserving white supremacy, prohibiting integration and miscegenation. James Ford Seale was incarcerated and died in 2011 in Terre Haute, Indiana federal prison.

The Good Book says, "Be not deceived, God is not mocked, for whatsoever a man soweth, that shall he also reap."

Moore and Dee went missing on May 1964, and were found in July, some forty days later by way of an accident. At the time, federal authorities had brought some two hundred sailors into Philadelphia, Mississippi to search for three missing civil rights workers, James Chaney, Michael (Mickey) Schwerner and Andrew Goodman.

One version is that a man was fishing in Louisiana and

saw a human torso in the tributary and notified the authorities in charge of the search. This place was almost one hundred and forty miles from Philadelphia, Mississippi. His action brought all searchers to this location. The man fishing must have been terrified at such a sighting in a place where he frequently fished.

The body part was examined but they didn't know if it was one of the three missing civil rights workers. There was no way to identify the body part. What they found was too mutilated to yield anything substantial, but they knew it was human. They also knew foul play was involved because it was weighted.

The next day, they found another body part more than half a mile away in the same body of water. They were still confused because they never found the third body. I was advised that they ultimately found an Alcorn University key in the pocket of Eddie Moore's torso.

The civil rights workers' bodies were later found under a huge pile of dirt from a pond that had been recently dug in Philadelphia, Mississippi.

At this point, the James Ford Seale name had not surfaced on the federal level as the main suspect in the murders of Moore and Dee. However, blacks in the Meadville area knew him as someone who was mean-spirited enough to commit the murders.

The word was, black people around Meadville and Bunkley said that James Ford Seale was terrible as a young individual. His hate for blacks was systemic. Blacks didn't deal with him, none of them trusted him and always tried to avoid his presence.

They saw him as a vicious racist ready to kill a black person at the drop of the hat. People in general believed that James Ford may have learned to hate blacks so profoundly from his daddy, Clyde, who was a staunch member of the Klan. Hate is taught, not birthed, which means someone drilled hate into James Ford's head.

Black people believed James Ford was criminally heinous and may have full involvement in numerous crimes against blacks outside of Franklin County. They said that James Ford was a very dangerous man with no heart or feelings of mercy for people he didn't like.

Charles Marcus Edwards caused Eddie Moore and Henry Dee to be picked up and ultimately killed. At the trial, he asked the judge for permission to speak to the Moore family, and it was granted.

It was stated that Edwards said, "I'm sorry for my involvement in the killings, and I want your forgiveness."

Thomas James responded, "I forgive you and God bless you." What a man, to be able to forgive after everything that happened to his brother.

Had it not been for Thomas James, the presence of a federal jury, prosecutor, Dunn Lampton, U.S. Attorney of the Southern District of Mississippi, Paige Fitzgerald, Special Litigation Council and trial attorney, Eric Gibson of Civil Rights Division of the Department of Justice, and the Federal Bureau of Investigation, James Ford Seale may have walked free again.

Also, because one of James Ford Seale's closest co-conspirators, Charles Marcus Edwards squealed on him to federal investigators to save himself from jail, Seale's dirty deeds finally caught up to him and justice was finally served.

Thomas James and David Ridgen were looking for information relegated towards developing a documentary of the Moore and Dee murders. That caused them to trek Franklin County, Mississippi near Meadville. For some reason, I am told, they stopped at a local business near Meadville.

Apparently, either Thomas James or David Ridgen indicated to an area person that they were looking for people that would share their thoughts on camera about the murders for their documentary. It is purported that one of them said to the person:

"It's too bad that James Ford Seale is dead, we would love to have had an opportunity to talk to him."

"James Ford Seale isn't dead," the individual quipped, "he's very much alive."

He made them aware of Seale's residence. They went there, found him sitting outside, and called out to him. He refused and rushed inside his house.

The discovery of James Ford Seale and the acknowledgement that the Homochitto Forest where Dee and Moore were beaten was a federal property was the new evidence that caused Seale to be federally tried.

It is said that, "He who laughs last laughs loudest."

Joe Lee Rollins, one of Moore's friends, said:

"I am very proud to have testified at Nub's (Moore's) trial, one of the finest and true friends I ever had. Nub was a guy that would not adversely pull a single hair from anyone's head. For him to end up maliciously murdered without provocation is racists beyond imagination. Nub was a great guy that respected everyone. He was my great friend."

Killing Blacks in Mississippi Was Easy

It is hard to believe that senators James Oliver Eastland and John C. Stennis were tight lipped during several killings of black people during their time in public office. They were against federal investigations of civil rights crimes and murders of blacks in Mississippi during their tenure. I would say their lack of action gave deference to the killings committed by the evil cabal.

Maybe Edgar Hoover, the first director of the Federal Bureau of Investigation of the United States, had agreed to a hands-off position in the civil rights of blacks in Mississippi to satisfy the senators. Hoover publicly stated that no FBI agents would be involved in the investigation or work on any civil rights activity in Mississippi.

I believe the plea for federal help should have come from Senators Eastland and Stennis, but nothing was said or done by either one.

As a matter of fact, Senator Eastland was in keen opposition to any form of integration in Mississippi and was openly opposed to it in the U.S. Senate for many years. Of course, there were adverse positions to integration harbored by other senators, many were democrats. They did not encourage people in the justice department to get involved in investigating black killings or civil rights in Mississippi. There were no landmark civil rights cases of record in Mississippi which nullified the use of state decisions.

Eastland and Stennis were very influential U.S. Senators in the state of Mississippi. Senator Eastland was a staunch and resolute conservative. This would have been fine as long as he would have been just with all of the people he represented. He had the power to make positive changes. He was President Temper and served in the Senate for thirty-six years. He was the voice of the white south, but an anathema for black folk. He said that blacks and whites should live in peace, but always separately and forever. The races should never come together in any venue whether socially, business, or educationally. He was racist and I think his record proves me right.

Senator Eastland was a major cotton producer and had over the years an array of blacks working for him. The blacks helped to make him richer by tilling his soil for cotton and harvesting the cotton that the fertile delta soil produced. The helpers were committed and worked the farm while he was in the U. S. Senate hating on the very people that worked his fields back home. The black population back home didn't even know he was working against their progress and freedom in Washington, D. C.

The more I read about Senator Eastland, the more I loathe the policies to which he espoused. He stepped on the constitution, kicked justice in the face and was known to have barricaded the path of progress for black people period. Justice for all was never a part of his agenda. He never intended, not once, to promote the cause of blacks in his entire career.

Eastland and Stennis had not just one chance to step up and say the killings of blacks by the Klan and other white people must stop, they had numerous opportunities to say enough is enough. However, they never said a word which means they didn't care how many blacks were killed.

The people said that even in Ruleville, Mississippi, Eastland's hometown, on June 26, 1964, a black man names Isaiah Taylor was killed by a white policeman during a traffic stop. The police stated that Taylor lunged at him with a knife and he shot and killed him to protect himself. There were no witnesses. Within a few days, the same policeman was laughing about the killing with friends as if it was a play thing. Blacks who knew the policeman and Taylor did not believe he was telling the truth. His dirty record of his past spoke for itself.

The people said that Ollie Shelby was shot and killed while in jail and no one was convicted, charged or suspended. The black community spoke of it only among themselves. It was business as usual after the killing in the town. Black people said there are huge accounts of blacks murdered in Mississippi by whites, but that was black talk around the fire places only and no one did anything about the killings.

In another instance, it is alleged that in 1958, Sheriff J. G. Treloar beat Woodrow Wilson Daniels almost to death in jail in Water Valley, Mississippi. They claimed Woodrow's wife bailed him out of jail and took him to the Memphis Hospital where he later died. After Treloar's trial, an all-white jury deliberated for twenty-eight minutes, and returned with a unanimous not guilty decision. Buster Treloar was cleared of all charges.

In 1963, I was advised that in Camden, Mississippi, a black man named Sylvester Maxwell was castrated and mutilated because he was black and defenseless. They found his mutilated body very close to a white family's home. His family, friends and the black community never got answers for his killing. They knew the drill, he was black and the Klan wanted him dead, and they killed him. Madison County was noted for many black murders that never were solved.

A black male named Ed Smith was killed in his yard by L. D. Clark while his wife watched. There was no provocation from Ed or anyone else in the house, yard or close by Clark. A short time later, it is purported that L. D. Clark bragged to friends about his killing of Smith and laughed at how he walked away complete free for the murder.

In 1959, it was said that in Clarksdale, Mississippi, a

fellow named Booker T. Mixon was murdered by the Klan. His naked body was found on the side of the road maliciously mutilated. The local police claimed it was a hit and run case. The black community contended it was hit by many Klan members and covered up by the local police department. They said that numerous automobiles would have had to run over Mixon many times to do that kind of damage.

The viciously ripped up body was a facsimile of the kind of damage that was done to blacks by the hands of the Klan. Limbs broken, face beaten beyond recognition, and body mutilated.

Black people in Coahoma County believed that more blacks were killed in that agrarian county than in any other county in Mississippi.

In Centreville Mississippi, Wilkerson County is connected to Adams on the north and Franklin on the east, two of the most vicious crime ridden counties in Mississippi by the Klan during the late fifties.

A black man named Samuel O'Quinn, hated by racists whites and the Klan, was killed because he stood up for what was right, spoke his piece and joined the NAACP. Racists whites labeled him as "an uppity nigger." They finally got a chance to do what they wanted to do for a long time. They shot and killed him in 1959. As usual, the killer was never found, and nothing was done about it.

The black community labeled it as a Klan murder. His death was not a shock to blacks because they knew he went to very dangerous places speaking justice.

A black man named Orsby was found in 1964 floating in the Black River in Pickens, Mississippi. He was wearing a CORE t-shirt. The killer was not identified and the black community felt the law enforcement's search was never seriously looked into because it is believed they already knew who the killer or killers were.

An off-duty constable killed Johnny Queen in Fayette, Mississippi in 1965. Johnny had not committed a crime or resisted an arrest. He had no gun, had not made a threat towards anyone. There was no reason for him to have been killed. His only problem was he was black and the constable wanted him dead. The constable walked away without a trial or conviction. No reason for the killing was ever given. The telling facts were the color of Queen's skin and the t-shirt he was wearing read, "It's time for a change."

In Crystal Spring, Mississippi, in 1966 it was said that a black man named Stewart was severely beaten while in police custody. The police claimed Stewart attempted to escape and the only way he could prevent his escape was to shoot and kill him. Think about it. He was severely beaten. Where did he get the strength to run away? A thinking man knows that he did not attempt to run.

What happened is the police beat him almost to death while he was handcuffed. They concocted the escape story to justify the murder. They weren't worried about a trial because they knew there would not be an investigation that would warrant an indictment. They needed a public justification for the shooting.

Had the situation been reversed, Senator Eastland would have led the fight against the black shooter and demanded justice and would have gotten it immediately. There was not a word from the two senators in the state of Mississippi in any of the murder cases.

In McComb, Mississippi, black people said Eli Brumfield on October 13, 9161, was stopped for speeding. The police said that Eli jumped from his car with a knife to attack him and was shot and killed by the police in self-defense. Nothing was done. The police office did not lose his job nor his gun, and he didn't have to go to trial. He was left on the police force to kill again.

The baffling thing that always got my dander up was the cavalier manner in which murders were handled or not handled at all by white sheriffs. Their attitudes were: "He's dead, I can't bring him back. Let the dead be dead and left alone so we can move on as usual."

A black person named Raspberry, who lived in Okolona, Mississippi and worked on a plantation, was shot and killed in 1965. The plantation owner became very upset with him and got his gun and shot and killed him. There is no record that the local sheriff even spoke to the plantation owner.

For some reason, certain white folk treated black folk as if they were non-domesticated animals. They felt totally at east about taking the life of a black person and went about their way as if they had killed a vicious animal.

Living through years of turmoil, strife, bigotry and

racism were Bailey and Susie Odell. Bailey Odell, whom I knew, was an exceptional individual, eagerly committed to the promotion of black people, schools, communities and his church. He was a man of principles and a high degree of integrity. Bailey was married to Susie Odell, a high school teacher at the Meadville colored school. Bailey and Susie were as close as two peas in a pod. When you saw one, you saw the other. They were an incredibly productive team that worked together on every endeavor. They paid incredible dues to the community and the people. They never flinched or held back on working with an issue.

Listening to Susie tell stories as to how difficult it was to maintain life economically when she first got out of college, was spellbinding. Being a teacher, you were not assured that at every payday you were going to get paid. There were times when a teacher was given a voucher to take to the store for the purchase of food and other small items until the next pay day. No matter how tough it was for them, they pushed ahead and taught the children.

Susie said, "When Bailey and I got married, things were still tough, but we stayed together and worked with the people and community. We suffered and helped others until things got better. Although better was not the best, we believed that a better day was coming, so we worked and waited."

Bailey was a strong supporter and overall good man. He could always be called on by any entity in the community to help out and he always responded positively. If the school roof leaked, Bailey Odell was called and it was repaired immediately. If a bus driver couldn't show up, they called Bailey Odell. If there were meetings that needed community input or a project that required support for passage, Bailey was there.

Black people said that the Bailey Odell legacy abruptly came to an end in the 1960s. He was bent over changing his automobile tire when James Ford Seale saw him and turned his speeding vehicle on him with a deadly velocity. Bailey never had a chance to escape and was killed instantly. The evil action of James Ford Seale cuffed out the life of another defenseless black man.

"I lost control of my vehicle and couldn't recover before it hit him," was Seale's story. In his response there was no remorse or apology to Susie or the community and no signs of regret.

People said that the killer was the same James Ford Seale that did the abduction and brutal murder of Henry Hezekiah Dee and Moore. The same James Ford Seale that was involved in the killing of Earl Hodges. Black folk were livid and emphatically believed that he killed Bailey Odell intentionally because of his hate for blacks.

Black people were right back where they had been since they set foot on the agrarian soil of Franklin County. They were helpless.

Nothing was done to refute the claim of Seale and, as usual, there was no extensive investigation. Even if there had been an investigation, the end result would have been the same, no charges against Seale because he was white and the victim was black.

No matter what Bailey Odell's life had been to the black community or how well known his name was in the white community, no white person was going to stand up and tell the sheriff to call in an outside authority for a fair and unbiased investigation. Seale was fee to kill without trepidation or being caught. After all, he went free for another forty-two years before being convicted for the Dee and Moore murders.

I wouldn't label all white people as unsympathetic. I believe their human factors was fear. White people were afraid of what the Klan would do to them if they stood up for blacks or for what was right.

At the time Bailey Odell was killed, there were hundreds of federal agents in Franklin and Adams counties because of the criminal activities of the Klan. However, the number of agents in Franklin could not stop the cross burnings at black homes and churches. The Klan just became more strategically planned, time sensitive, and secretive.

The Klan was an adhesive group of misfits that espoused to gross rogue unsavory tendencies. Their biggest fears and deepest concerns were losing their white women to black men and the integration of schools where black boys would have access to white girls every day. They figured white girls would learn that black boys were human and that every negative thing that white men had purported about black men were lies and that the only difference between black and white men is the color of their skin. They were also equally bent on keeping black people from a quality educational system and enhancing their cognitive skills.

White men could have relationships with black women, that was all right, but the opposite was sure death.

Reverend Clyde Briggs was a real asset to the community. I know because I was one of the young people that he helped get into college. They tried their best to assassinate him for trying to help black children.

Had it not been for Reverend Briggs, I probably would not have seen the inside of college walls. He was my only chance. He was very vigilant in helping me. He came to my house looking for me to take me to college. I didn't even know he was coming.

I was shocked later on when I learned Reverend Briggs had to outrun Klan members in his car and blow the horn in distress to warn his wife to open the door in fear of getting shot.

All the Reverend wanted was to help black students obtain the same college opportunities as the whites. Cutting logs, paper-wood, and farming were not the choices of all black students. Many of them wanted to go to college.

Ebbert Briggs was a powerful black man in the community. He worked on the railroad and never bothered anyone, but didn't take any pushing around from white people. I guess the Klan got the word that Ebbert was one of the leaders in the black community and they burned down his house. Ebbert sent out the word that he was going to rebuild his home and dared anyone to come out and try to stop him or do anything to the structure during the rebuilding. If so, everyone would know who was on his property because they would not walk away but would be carried away. He rebuilt his house and it still stands today.

The Klan burned a cross in front of my godfather, Dan Adams's house, and it frightened him. The next morning, he went to the sheriff's office and told him what happened. The sheriff said that the cross burning was not meant for him. That was a clear indication that the sheriff knew what was going on and who was doing the burning.

Apparently, the cross burning was meant for my brother A. J. He sent the word out that if a cross was burned in front of his house, everyone was going to know who burned it because he would leave him dead right by the burning cross. No cross was ever burned in front of his house.

The word was out that the Klan was going to kill A. J. Smith and that was enough to alarm the entire black community. However, A. J. was not afraid or alarmed by the Klan in spite of their roguish history. His position was, if they try to kill me, they better not miss, because they will not get a second chance. A. J. Could kill a running rabbit with a single shot rifle. He didn't stop driving the log truck and he didn't stop going where ever he wanted to go, day or night. He was never bothered by the Klan.

Ranken McDaniel's mother and my mom were two sibling's children. Ranken was an uneducated, unpolished young man that was well-mannered and always did the right thing. He never got into trouble with anyone that I know of or heard anyone say he bothered anything that did not belong to him. He worked hard to take care of himself and to help his parents, Sam and Dean.

Sam and Dean were good parents to all their children. They took them to church and brought them up in the right way. All of their children had great respect for all people, and were always on their best behavior. If no one harmed them, they harmed no one.

Even though there were hundreds of black youngsters that turned out to be great, with impeccable records of doing the right thing, some turned up dead and their families never found out who killed them or why. This is what happened to Ranken McDaniel.

Sam and Dean died and there was never an investigation or even a quality look into the death of their son. After the death of Ranken, the comments from black people in the community were basically the same, the Klan killed him and the killer will never be found.

On this particular day in Bude, Mississippi, this white man attempted to beat up this black man in the black part of town. The black man gave the white man a well-deserved beating that he didn't expect and would remember for the rest of his life. Then he did the safe thing. He walked between some nearby houses to John Clark's place before the white guy could come back with his white crowd of friends and had someone drive him to New Orleans where he stayed with relatives.

Getting out of town was the right and safe thing for him to do. Had he stayed, one of two things would have happened. Either the sheriff would have locked him up and Klan members would have been allowed into the jail that night to beat him to death, or the crowd of white men would have come back, snatched him up and taken him deep into the woods to beat him to death or left him hanging by the neck to a tree. One thing was for sure, he was going to be killed one way or the other.

There was another black man named Rassey Hunt who didn't want to work one Saturday. He came into Meadville as people did on Saturday to shop and see friends who usually came to town. The fellow that he worked for was angry and came to town and found Rassey at Joe Johnson's Cafe. He came huffing and puffing and ordered Rassey outside where he was going to take him back to work on the farm.

Rassey said he would go outside because he didn't want to cause problems in Joe Johnson's business. As Rassey walked out the door, the white guy kicked him. Rassey turned around and hit the man with a blinding left hook, causing him to land on the ground. The guy got up and they started throwing hard and heavy punches on one another.

Some white people driving by stopped, jumped out of their cars to help the white guy. He stopped fighting Rassey and said:

"This is my fight, not yours. Get in your cars and go. If I can't win my fight alone, I don't want your help."

The whites left and he and Rassey started fighting all

over again. Both were bloody. Finally, Joe Johnson stepped in and got them to stop. The white guy got into his truck and left. Joe Johnson took Rassey into his cafe and cleaned him up, but Rassey didn't leave the cafe. The people around him thought the white man would return with his gun to shoot Rassey, but he didn't come back.

Rassey told people around him that he was going back to work for the guy on Monday morning and that he has always lived in Franklin County and was not leaving. He was lucky he fought with a white man and won, and there wasn't a retaliation because the white man was honest and not a racist, otherwise Rassey would have been in serious trouble.

I was a senior in high school and had played baseball and basketball since eighth grade. We were on our way to play a game in Rodney, Mississippi when one of our cars was stopped by a state police just north of Fayette, Mississippi in Jefferson County. Our third baseman, Phillip Byrd, was in the car. All of the boys were ordered out of the car and apparently, the patrolman didn't like Phillip's attitude because he didn't move as fast as he wanted. The patrolman called Phillip a "smarty nigger" and pulled out his blackjack and commenced to beat him in the face and on the head. Then he handcuffed Phillip and put him in his car and took him to jail. Our coach bailed Phillip out for resisting arrest, a crime he did not commit.

There was another white highway patrolman whose jurisdiction covered highway #84 between highway #61 and #51. That fellow just loved to beat up on black drivers, just because he had a gun and badge.

Myron Lindsey was a truck driver who had a regular run from Roxie to Meadville. He was stopped by this rogue patrolman called Allred for what he said was speeding. Allred had a lot of people taking about how dirty he was and what he did to black drivers. He never stopped white drivers no matter what they did on the road.

Myron told Allred he drove that road regularly and knew the speed limit and always stayed within the limit because he didn't want a ticket or trouble with the law.

Allred asked Myron if he was calling him a liar. He knew that

Myron was not going to agree to that. He just wanted to harass him because he had the upper hand.

"No sir, I respect your badge and you as an officer of the law. I would never disrespect your position and call you a liar. If you say I was speeding, write the ticket. I'll give it to my job." Myron said the patrolman called him "a nigger" and commenced to beat him over the head and in the face as he cursed him.

Finally, he stopped beating him, wrote him a ticket, threw it at him and told him to pay it immediately. I happened to be in Meadville at the time and saw Myron's face and the results of the blows he took.

Myron was not the only driver that a patrolman beat up on that same highway. A patrolman named Beasley had a habit of beating blacks.

Another friend of mine had several run-ins with Beasley

in particular. My friend lived in Roxie. He didn't want his name used in his statement as to what the patrolman did to him. He said he was driving alone on the road between Meadville and Roxie, Mississippi when Beasley tried to stop him. He continued driving because he knew Beasley's reputation of brutality on blacks, and a chase ensued.

My friend had a hopped-up car that was fast. Beasley knew where he lived and went to his address where he found my friend's father waiting on the porch. Beasley told his father that he came to get his son. His father told Beasley that his son was in the house, but no one was coming inside to get anyone. He told him that the smart thing for him to do was to leave his house.

Huffing and puffing, Beasley eventually left. Sometime later, my friend went to Meadville to pay a bill. He was seen entering the place of business. As he left, he was arrested and placed in jail. His mother went to the jail, paid his fine and was told that her son would be released. The word came that he was going to be taken from the jail and killed by the Klan. In the middle of the night, he was taken out of jail and into the woods along with another black man who whispered to him:

"While they're beating you, if they tell you to run at any time, don't, but fall to the ground and play dead. If you run, they'll shoot you."

They beat him nearly unconscious and one at a time, walked up to him and asked:

"Do you know me?"

He told them he didn't know anyone. They continued to beat him until they thought he was dead and they left him. Sometime before daybreak, he garnered enough strength to crawl through the woods for what seemed to be miles to the main road. Earlier in the day, he emerged from the woods and flagged down a car. The driver happened to be a friend who he recognized. He was driven home.

While at home, he packed some things to leave Roxie. Several men held a bit of trepidation about driving him out of town. There was a business woman in their mix who agreed to drive him where he wanted to go. She put him in her car and the men drove behind her to a safe connection to Chicago. He remained in Chicago for years until it was safe to return.

I was blessed because I drove and hitched that highway for years and never was detained by Beasley or Allred or anyone else. I carried a gun every day, and I made sure I followed all the safety rules. I am so grateful I didn't get stopped because I was not going to take a beating from anyone. I would take a traffic ticket without a word, but not a single blow would I take from anyone.

My mother worried about me all the time and eventually I finally understood why. I knew race relationships were bad and I knew that black people were always wrong no matter how right they were when white people were involved. But what I didn't understand was certain white people were always around whose primary goal was to figure out how to get young black people into trouble so they could take advantage and use them for their purposes.

I began to think analytically about situations that could pose a problem for me because I was thinking on a different level than what was the usual mindset in the black community. Because of exposure to the civil rights movement, national news, radio news, newspapers, embellished education, my thinking was elevated to a new paradigm, and I figured out how to avoid getting into trouble altogether.

For instance, when I wanted to go home for the weekend, when is the best time to drive one hundred and fifteen miles? Instead of leaving late evening and getting home in the late night, I would wait until the next morning and leave early and be on the road during the day. Instead of stopping on the way for food, I would make a sandwich. Instead of driving the full speed limit, I would drive ten miles slower. Instead of driving through towns, I would drive around them if there was another road.

I would never pull into a rest stop. I would stop along the highway for a few minutes to stretch and walk around the car. I would never turn off the motor. The worst thing that could happen is the car would not start up again. I would be stuck at the mercy of people I didn't know and who probably wouldn't care about my predicament.

The older I became, the more I understood that we live in a white world with many racists who got special concessions for their harmful aggressions toward blacks because they were white and the law didn't apply to them. I don't ever remember a white man going to jail for anything he did to a black person.

I also thought about what could've happened to me as I hitched rides from Kirby to Prentiss and back to Meadville and Natchez, Alcorn, Vicksburg, and the Delta. I realized how blessed I was that nothing happened to me. God was listening and answered my mother's prayers, and I survived the kills of Mississippi. Every now and then, blacks got a break.

In 1959, the civil rights activities were heating up in Mississippi, and I had just graduated from Alcorn State University. I got a job with the Madison County board of Education. My headquarters was in Canton, Mississippi, but I worked at Madison, Mississippi, twenty miles away.

Medgar Evers and others were heating up the civil rights movement in Jackson, Mississippi and I wanted to be involved. Martin Luther King came to Jackson and I was euphoric to get involved in the movement. I showed up at the rally and listened to Dr. King electrify the crowd with his speech. It was one of the happiest days of my life. I could see enormous opportunities for progress for black people if we stayed together, got registered, voted, and pushed against the system.

Shortly after that meeting, I went home to see my mother and got the shock of my life. Her face was strained and I knew something was grossly wrong from her mannerism. I asked her:

"Mama you know I know your every mood. I know when things are right or wrong with you, so tell me what's wrong."

She hesitated, before speaking:

"I want you out of Mississippi, and I want you out now. I don't want someone to come and tell me that the white folk have killed you!"

I knew that she meant the Klan because she had heard about what happened to other blacks in the state and the thought of me being killed had upset her.

When I heard what she said, I became grossly upset because I didn't want to leave Robby, the girl I had met. I was having the best time of my life and leaving was not in my plan under any circumstances.

Mama's words were paramount, without question. Whatever Mama wanted she got, from all of us, no discussions, no negotiations, or trepidation, just vigilance toward her position with dispatch. I couldn't think of saying "no" to Mama, nor telling her that I couldn't leave. I got in my car right then and drove to where I was staying, packed my things, put them in my car and drove to Robby's parents' home.

Robby was out of town, and I knew it, but I asked her mother to inform her that I was going to Chicago. I really didn't plan to stay in Chicago. I intended to make some money and come back to Mississippi and marry Robby and take her back to Chicago to live. Things didn't work out as I had planned. I stayed in Chicago for two years without going back to Mississippi and I lost Robby. My life took on an entirely different direction.

Ten years later, I met another fantastic young lady. I

knew immediately she was the one for me. I ended up marrying her and she has proven to be one of the best decisions that I have ever made. She is not only smart, but also the essence of pulchritude.

Mama didn't make impetus decisions. She thought things out in details about me and what I should do to avoid mistakes with my life. Her overwhelming concern was fear for my life and her action may have saved me. I had penetrating pain from leaving Robby, but I got over it when I met the Chicago girl.

I thought to myself, I hope I can live long enough to see mean white people brought down from their self-proclaimed lofty status of superiority. I want to live to see black people live in a system of equality and fairness and where there will be no more white killings of black just because they are black.

As I think of Mama's concern to get me out of Mississippi, I now appreciate her forcing me out as badly as it hurt me to leave on the spur of the moment. I knew things were dangerous for young blacks, but I really didn't understand the full magnitude of the adversities facing me and the acute racism that existed at the time. I thought staying in my lane and not going around trouble spots was my sanctuary. I didn't think of the calamity that would come looking for me. I wouldn't start trouble but I would protect myself if trouble came after me. No one was going to drag me from my car and into the woods and hang me without some of the aggressors being victims of fire from my gun.

I wouldn't know who they were or how many, but I did understand what they had done to black folk in the past. The gun I carried every day was going to be used to protect and save my life. Not to do harm to another just because I had a gun. I was a well-mannered good guy with values, character, integrity and morality. But I would protect myself from bad guys and I wouldn't hesitate for a second.

Losing Minnie Lee was a Crushing Blow

The first stop on my agenda after arriving home in Mississippi was always Mama's house. The second stop was the Rollins' home because that was the home of my dearest friend, Minnie Lee Rollins.

Minnie Lee Rollins was a beautiful young black woman with all of the accessories that go with a complete statuesque woman. She was a show stopper, miss gorgeous and she knew it but was not a flaunter. She was always calm and quiet, a non-gregarious person in public presence, but when she and I got together, she would talk and kid around nonstop. It appeared that she saved up all her funny things and long conversations until I came home so she could let it all out on me.

We would just hang out for hours and hours and have fun doing nothing but being together. We spent so much time together. When I was home, she would drop everything, including her boyfriend, who I knew, and give me all of her time. I just loved having her with me.

Minnie and my mother got along so well as if she was a member of my family. Her mom and dad were very nice, and it was always great to sit and talk to them along with Minnie.

When I was a young boy, Minnie's dad drove an ice truck and brought ice to our house. He used to chase me around, catch and tickle me, pull my ears, rub my head and hold me by the seat of my pants to keep me from getting away. Before he would drive off, he would give me that candy bar or those cookies he had in his truck. Minnie and I became inseparable friends.

There weren't many places of entertainment, only John Clark's and Son Peaches' places in Bude. We would drive to Brookhaven or Natchez to eat at the Savoy Grill or go down by the Mississippi River and watch the boats. We would also go across the Natchez bridge into Vidalia or to Haney's Big House in Ferriday, Louisiana. Those places would be loaded with people on the weekend, many of them from out our way.

Being with Minnie was so much fun, we didn't need places of entertainment. We could drive around on the Bunkley Road and stretch out under a big shade tree or ride out on the McNai Road by my house and sit around and talk. She was so bright and agile, always with interesting things to talk about. Her boyfriend was a lucky fellow to be in a relationship with her.

The last time we were together, I had this different kind of feeling that I'd never had before. It was like I didn't want to leave her for some reason. I was being sent to California for training and knew I would be going overseas shortly after, and it was going to be two years before I would be coming home again. Something inside me seemed to want to bring her with me. I didn't express my feelings to her.

It was very late as I was driving her home and she was so quiet. That was very unusual. I had never seen her that somber before. I had never seen her cry, sad or unhappy. She was always jubilant when I was around.

With me, it wasn't like being in love and leaving the person that I loved. I was sick, and there wasn't a medicine to cure the feeling. I told her:

"Nothing hurts as the pain of not being with you tomorrow. I won't be here. I'll be eighteen hundred miles away, and it will be a long time before I see you again. I will be going overseas immediately after training and you can rest for sure that I will write you once every week and if I don't hear from you every week, I will find a means to get away and come home and get you and take you back with me where I will have you with me every day. I don't know what you will do with that boyfriend of yours, but you will be with me."

She didn't say a word, and her mood became more somber and still no words. "What's wrong Minnie Mouse?" As I sometimes teased her. She broke down crying profusely and

I pulled to the side of the road and stopped.

"Now wait a minute. What did I do to you to make you so sad?" I asked.

I sat there for a while and let her cry it all out. I was trying to figure out what to say to her to calm her down to get to the bottom of what had her lamenting in such an astonishing manner.

"It would be nice if you would tell me what I've done to you to make you sad enough to cry. I can't stand tears. They make me sad and I don't think you want me to start crying too," I said.

"I don't want you to go, I don't want you to leave me. I get the feeling that you may never come back. I don't have another friend as genuine as you." She said with both arms around me.

"Nonsense, I will come back, and if you drop me while I'm away, I'll scream to the top of my voice and fall to the ground kicking and yelling. I will be back, and you better be waiting for me with open arms. You will always be my special friend, and I'll be back to you, don't worry. My time will pass so fast and I will be out and back home and we will be together again."

Almost three years later, I came home and ran into her in a store in Meadville. The sight of me caught her by surprise and for a second, she froze in her position. Then she ran to me and we embraced in the isle of the store.

"You didn't tell me you were coming home. You left me completely in the dark."

We went outside and hugged. She was just as beautiful as ever and just as shapely. Three years older had not adversely affected her body, face and apparently her feeling toward me in the least. My old feeling for her was still the same, but I knew our relationship as it once was had to stop.

"I got your letter informing me that you were getting married. You know I cried profusely. I was so sad, no I'm still sad. Just kidding, but, really, I'm happy for you because I know you have a good man and you're happy."

I stopped writing her because I didn't want it to be frustrating for me or her.

"Even though he's a good man, I miss you so much, and it has not been happy as it was between you and me. I cried for days knowing that we can't spend all the time together as we used to, but we will still be able to spend time together. I got that commitment from my husband before we were married. You were the strong reservation against me getting married. I really didn't want to leave you single and me getting married. It was a bothersome thing for me. I really didn't want to do it, but it was time and he is such a nice guy, but he isn't you. Had you asked me to wait, I would have. I would have loved to have been married to you for life. He said I can still spend time with you."

"How could you ask him for us to still get together?"

"When we were talking about the guidelines of the marriage, I told him that I only had one thing I didn't want to change. He said we don't have to talk about it, I know what it is and you can have it as always. I know you want to spend time with your friend Eddie. You all getting together is fine with me, that's not a problem."

I didn't stay in Mississippi long. We got together a couple of times before I left for Chicago. Leaving her caused me a huge state of pathos. Adjusting to her being married was a problem. She was constantly on my mind. I had no one at home that could keep me happy every day, all day.

Not too long into her marriage, she was killed supposedly in a car accident. She was already buried when I got the news of her death. I was devastated. I was so distraught that had I known about her funeral, I wouldn't have had the strength to attend the service. I couldn't have contained myself. It would have been too much for me to absorb and my action would have been troublesome for the family.

Finally, I went home, and my brother, A. J. took me to see her burned-out car. People were saying that the car was not damaged badly enough for her to be killed.

When I saw her car, my legs weakened, perspiration pushed through the pores of my skin. I began to tremble, my throat tightened, my eyes welled up and my hands were shaking.

I leaned against the wreckage of the car with my head down for a resurgence of strength. I could not stand on my own feet without the help of a crutch.

A. J. probably saw my reaction and didn't want to see me in that state. He walked to the other side of the burned-out car as if he had not seen it before. He had only seen me really down at the funeral of my mother and at that funeral, everyone was down.

I felt like agreeing with the skeptics. I didn't want to believe she died in that car. From what I understood, no one saw her body after the accident. The funeral home personnel would not allow anyone, not even her husband or a relative, to see what was supposed to be her body. I found that to be very strange. I don't think a funeral home had that kind of power.

Her parents and husband were probably extremely distraught and could not think logically at the time and did not push to see the body.

All I can say is, I miss my friend terribly when I go home, and I would very much like to know what really happened to her. She was the best friend I ever had. I never was able to garner the facts as to what really happened to her. However, I will love her until I leave the face of the earth - that's what she meant to me.

Black Pillars in the Local Community

Laura Adams cooked in the Mt. Olive High School lunch room for years. She was an Eastern Star in Mt. Olive Baptist Church and a member of the local school board.

Lula Adams was a strong voice in the amen section at Mt. Olive church. She would pitch the hymn and the rest of the church joined in with harmony. She had that foot stomping that was only applicable to Mt. Olive Church.

Ernest Brown was the Vocational Agricultural teacher, a role model, with very high principles and always sang during high school chapel service.

Juanita Brown, the first black teacher in the Franklin County integrated school system, was a superb teacher and church member. She was involved in voter registration, democratic politics, and worked on election day.

Samuel Brown was a veteran, college trained plumber,

promoted voter registration, and a member of the democratic party. In 1971, he ran for sheriff in Franklin County. He was advised to move his family out of Franklin when it was rumored that the Klan might be targeting him to be killed for his strong stance on civil rights. He refused to run and said that he would defend his family at all cost and would not stop his involvement in black political activities.

Henry Byrd was involved in the community. Whatever he was called upon to do, he did it and he didn't hesitate. He participated in the building of the original Mt. Olive church along with Robert Smith and others.

Johnny Fells walked about eight miles to church on Sundays and would help to do whatever needed to be done to make the services go smoothly and would walk back home if he didn't get a ride. He was a wonderful person and a real gentleman. He believed in the political system and that black people should be allowed to vote and he worked to make that possible. He lived by himself and walked miles along the road alone. He never feared the Klan and they never bothered him or his house.

Joe Green was a railroad man, a Mason, and gravedigger. He and his wife, Doll, took in elderly sick people and cared for them as long as they lived. Doll was an Eastern Star, usher in the church, chaperone for school children and strong church member. Joe was keen on church and Sunday school, and was a community advocate. They were real assets to the community.

Dave and Ella Hodges were excellent Sunday school

teachers and dedicated to their local church. Dave was a good family man and both were concerned about their community.

Nig Hunt was always a good community person and was available to help those in need. He became a Christian as an old man and one of the Sunday school's best teachers. He was also highly respected for his commitment to the church.

Mrs. Amy Johnson visited the sick, would sit with them and helped where she was needed. She was a strong Christian and responsible person. She loved to fish and walked long distances to her favorite fishing spots. She fished alone most of the time and fishing long hours didn't bother her even if the fish weren't biting.

Joe Johnson was the first black businessman in Meadville proper. He, along with his wife Maggie, owned a restaurant. Joe was an accepted promoter of republican politics with certain white politicians. He actually campaigned for republican candidates. He never experienced violence for being involved.

Monroe Johnson encouraged young people in education, was a role model, helped in the community, and helped others.

Walter McGhee was an agriculture teacher who encouraged students to stay in school, go to college and get the best education possible. He wanted children to prepare themselves for the future. He would take them to Alcorn State University so they could get a feel for the college atmosphere.

J. L. Miller was a veteran, basketball volunteer coach, who volunteered in the school and chaperoned on school trips. He was great with the children and was an excellent role model for the students. In church, he sometimes directed the choir.

Leslie Miller, secretary of Mt. Olive church for years, Eastern Star, great cook for church functions and involved in local school activities.

Mrs. Elvira Smith was an Eastern Star, church helper, community-minded and excellent person. She was the mother of twelve children and was committed to helping where she was needed.

Robert Smith, helped build the first Mt. Olive church and gave people food during their difficult times. He was a very concerned community person with a big heart.

Carey Tillman, a veteran, great Sunday school teacher, bright fellow, good organizer and family man.

Mattie Tillman, a church usher, Eastern Star, school participant and helped with the sick. She was the wife of Carey Tillman.

Amos Webster bought the first school bus that transported black children to Mt. Olive School. Children came from White Apple, Roxie, Hamburg, and the Oldenburg areas. Amos was an excellent businessman and a great family man.

Dan Adams taught the teenagers in the community how to drive on his old log truck. On Saturdays, he gave us the price of the movie.

These people had an indelible imprint on my life. They were the people that I looked up to and respected. They taught me in Sunday school and gave me a chance to challenge them in discussions. They gave me rides to Natchez, Meadville, and Roxie, and money for the Saturday matinee. They were the father I didn't have and the shield I needed to grow up under real leadership.

It was their guidance that helped to structure the foundation of my life. They were the people that didn't tell me how to live and be a good person, they showed me. To me, they were the greatest. I am eternally grateful to each and every one of them for their commitment to me. They will always be a part of my life.

White Pillars in the Local Community

Dr. Walter Costley took care of all his patients, black and white, with the same quality of care. Many of his black patients at times had no money, but he never withheld his professional services. He would take a pound of butter, a dozen of eggs and promises of, "I'll pay you when I get the money." Inclement weather did not stop him from getting to his patients. He walked through mud, water, and plowed fields to care for black patients who were sick and had no money.

Garveese Dillion ran a good business and gave great respect to all of his customers. He greeted everyone cordially, and whoever stepped up to the counter first, was taken care of. Everyone received the same quality of service.

Carey Graves was the president of the Bank of Franklin, a true business professional. He ran an excellent bank that served the public. His job was to promote the bank, serve the customers and to create an atmosphere that caused all the public to want to do business with the bank. He did it well and was successful at this profession.

Tom Halford was a small store owner at the entrance of the city. He was a quiet man, but ran a good one-man store. Didn't matter if the customer was black or white, young or old, they received the same special treatment. He was appreciated by the town and his customers.

John and Lin Hollinger were businessmen in Meadville. They co-signed my papers to get a loan to pay for my last year in college. They were aware that my mother was very sick and may not recover, but that didn't bother them. They did not ask a single question when I told them my mother said for them to sign the papers for the loan. The loan was approved and the money was sent directly to the college. Years later, the Franklin Advocate wrote an article on my political activities in Chicago. Subsequently, I returned home and went to their store to say thanks. They commended me on the job I was doing in Chicago and were happy that they were able to help.

Mayes McGhee was a very fair and credible lawyer. He represented his clients with professionalism. He believed in doing the right thing and through his legal responsibilities, he promoted a good professional picture for the town of Meadville. He had an outstanding history of superb legal work, integrity and character.

Mrs. Hester McLemore ran a store in Kirby. Her first

location was situated near the railroad track where the trains stop to take on water. There was a spur where rail cars were dropped off to be loaded with paper-wood to be taken to the paper mill in Natchez, Mississippi. Many blacks had credit in her store. If someone got behind with their bill, she never yelled at them, but sat them down and helped them get back in good standing. She earned respect in the black community for being kind and fair to black people.

Quitman McLemore was a businessman in Meadville and son of Mrs. Hester McLemore. He was one of the four co-signers on my papers to borrow the money I needed to finish my last year in college. He also knew Mama was very ill, but he signed the papers because he respected my mother.

Mack McLemore was the son of Mrs. Hester McLemore and brother of Quitman McLemore. He ran a logging business and was not going to mistreat anyone, no matter their color. If a black person was with him, no one else was going to mistreat that person. He believed in doing the right thing. He loved baseball and often went to Cotton league games and took several black people with him to see the Natchez team play. Blacks sat with him in the bleachers, ate the same food and anyone who attempted to bother or stop him, was dealt with. He was not going to tolerate adverse treatment of blacks that were with him or worked for him.

Bill Scarborough was an automobile dealer in Meadville. He was a respected businessman for his fair practices with all of his customers. He was also a good person with integrity and responsibility. He didn't cheat black people or treat them as second-class citizens. A man was a man and a customer a customer. When he walked into the bank, he took his place in the line and waited for service just as everyone else.

Callie Scott was unusual. She was always helping black people and would go to great length to help. She didn't care what people said about what she was doing. It didn't matter to her. She always helped people, some who were black, sick and poor. Everyone knew her and people talked about her, but she continued for years.

E. B. Seale was also a businessman in Meadville and was the fourth co-signer on my loan papers to borrow the money to pay for my senior year in college. All of the businessmen signed my loan papers because of my mother's record of character and integrity. She always kept her word.

Those store owners believed in her, and they had no trepidation about taking a chance with her. I had to repay the loan, and I paid it without a hitch. My mother did recover.

C. O. Twiner owned land out on the McNair Road. My mom wanted to build a house. She liked a spot not too far from his store. She spoke to him about purchasing an acre from him. She told him that she didn't have all the money at the time for what the land was worth. He told her he would survey the land and whatever she could afford at the time, to bring it to him and the land would be hers. He gave her the land and later, she had her house built there. He was a good man and he knew she would eventually pay him.

James Wentworth was a fair businessman, a good citizen and a credit to the town. There was never an adverse word written or promoted against him. He was highly respected and ran a good business.

Luther Whittington was a sawmill and land owner. He did not have an adverse connotation of blacks as many others did. Blacks lived on his land, and grew crops for themselves. They also worked at his sawmill along with white employees, and they all got along because of his leadership. He treated all employees the same, and was highly respected by all that worked for him.

Sue Smith was a kind woman who helped me bring closure to the killings of Moore and Dee by taking me to the exact location in the woods where the beatings took place. That allowed me to find solace from the piercing pain that caused my heart to throb.

Someone is going to question why I have written about some white people in a county where many innocent black people have been killed, and only one white person has ever gone to jail for murdering a black. My response is simple. I feel the white people that I have listed are people whose names are worthy of being mentioned here. They have earned their place in this book because of their lives of respect, decency, character, integrity, responsibility and accountability. They harbored no visible traits of racism, bigotry or superiority complex toward blacks.

Of course, they lived within the confines of adverse

custom and traditions to black people. However, they did not create those conditions, and they didn't join those who promoted the status quo. Their nature would not allow them to do or say anything adverse to the right thing toward blacks or being a party to anything that was viciously done to or against black people. Their character spoke volumes and elevated my understanding of white people around me. I was glad to discover that such people lived in the county in which I grew up.

Moving Forward

With a multiplicity of terrible things that could have happened to me, I know that I am blessed to still be alive. I continue to love going home to Mississippi where I grew up and enjoyed some of the best years of my life.

In spite of the many horrendous tragedies that took place, there is still something intriguing about Meadville that continuously beckons me, and I am always eager to yield.

I guess it is the trove of positive personal experiences I remember that surpasses the bad ones. It is the good times I spent with Minnie Lee Rollins and B. J. Hunt with his gregarious personality, and the fun times we had with Hargie Ann David and Lillian Litterton. It's the rabbit, squirrel, and deer hunting and other enjoyable times with my brothers A. J., Albert, and James.

It is the fishing trips for years on the Morgan Folk Creek and the May branch and ponds, and Homochitto River, and

Horse Shoe Lake and the back waters of Lake Pontchartrain with my niece Jewel.

It is the beautiful trees and rolling hills, the babbling springs and the growing up among people that cared for each other. It's my Sunday school days and Mt. Olive Church services.

It's the memory of my mother and the long talks we shared sitting around the house. It's the caring and sharing with each other and the comradery that ran from house to house.

It is my old high school days with Ford Mason, Felix Jones, Elvia Brown, W. F. Green, and our commitment to be good students and class leaders. It's remembering the smart students such as Jo Frances Thomas, Mozell (MI.) Williams, Ruby Lee Wilson, JoAnn Green, Yvonne Smith, Susie Bell Parker, Eloise Byrd that made up those lively crowds at basketball games, and other events. The fervent thoughts of Betty Byrd, Ethel Lee Smith, Henry (Dude) Smith and Ephraim (Mouse) Smith, I can never forget. They are imprinted in my brain.

When I think of the good friends and relatives of mine, I know I am one lucky and blessed fellow. I was poor and at the bottom of the economic barrel, but that did not matter to anyone close to me, and it made no difference in relationships with others whatsoever.

Things have changed drastically in certain disciplines. The people are different and better educated. They are in a more acceptable mode of other people, black and white. The community is still not flawless, but the degree of understanding and tolerance has seen a spike in growth.

Law and justice have virtually supplanted the Klan, and killings of blacks cannot happen without a stiff price in justice. There is character and integrity and, yes morality in the town's law enforcement. If such crimes take place, they are highly camouflaged and sporadically committed. The changes are appreciable, and have been good for all the people and town. Most people have accepted the changes and moved ahead.

Money in the school system is no longer spent on two different high schools, blacks and whites are in one high school for equal education without conflict. White and black children are taught by black and white teachers. Black and white children play together and if there are conflicts, they settle them among themselves. Parents or other adults do not get involved. The children remain friends and still play together.

I marveled when my cousin came to the family reunion with his white wife and brown children. I get the same feeling when I visit the courthouse and see blacks as office workers and law enforcement officers. You go into the bank and see black and white employees working beside each other. The credible progressive changes are fungible without extrapolated internal conflicts.

It is easy to see that in Meadville relationships have softened and overt racism and bigotry is no longer apparent. That alone is enough to make me want to visit home. Even without my friends, it's still a pleasure going home and walking on the ground on which I grew up.

Now white people around Meadville drive past black people and wave. When they are in voice distance, they speak. Blacks don't have to get off the sidewalk when white people approach. You immediately know that things have changed when you see white women holding hands with a black husband and their mixed children tagging along and everyone seems to be at peace.

The town is not a standard of measurement for equality. However, it no longer has the remnant of, "If you white, you all right. If you black, get back."

Blacks are no longer relegated as inferiors just because they are black, and public negative connotations toward them are either jettisoned or muted in public sectors. It is "yes" or "no" as blacks stand or sit and look white people in the eyes and converse, and their hands aren't behind them as they present themselves as strong black people.

The pinnacle of justice has not been reached and there are miles to go. As horrific as the murders of A. D. Brown, Henry Hezekiah Dee, Eddie Charles Moore, Johnny Nix, Ranken McDaniel and Bailey Odell were, hopes have become swizzles of improvements in race relationships. The brutality they suffered will never happen to another black person in Franklin County. Now there are just laws by which all criminals will be judged.

The good old boys' system that once allowed bad guys to skirt and evade laws and stay out of jail no longer exist. Now Meadville, Mississippi is:

"A place of peace."

www.ingramcontent.com/pod-product-compliance
Lightning Source LLC
Chambersburg PA
CBHW060211050426
42446CB00013B/3048